RAND McNALLY

DISCOVERY ATLAS OF THE WORLD

Hornbill

Cape Buffalo

Hippopotamus

Zebra

Lion

Eland

Python

Wildebeest

Cheetah

Impala

Ostrich

Rand McNally for Kids™

Books•Maps•Atlases

Peafowl

Gibbon

Cobra

Discovery Atlas of the World

General manager: Russell L. Voisin
Executive editor: Jon M. Leverenz
Editor: Elizabeth Fagan Adelman
Production editor: Laura C. Schmidt
Manufacturing planner: Marianne Abraham

Discovery Atlas of the World
Copyright © 1993 by Rand McNally & Company
Published and printed in the United States of America

Portions of this book were originally published in Rand McNally *Children's World Atlas,* copyright © 1992, 1991 by Rand McNally. Every effort has been made to trace the copyright holders of the photographs in this publication. Rand McNally apologizes in advance for any unintentional omissions and would be pleased to insert the appropriate acknowledgment in any subsequent edition of this book.

Library of Congress Cataloging-in-Publication Data

Rand McNally and Company.
    Discovery atlas of the world.
        p.   cm.
    At head of title: Rand McNally.
    Includes index.
    Summary: Features twenty-five pictorial maps showing terrain, animals, people, cities, and countries for each continent. Also includes illustrations of the characteristics of the regions.
    ISBN 0-528-83577-7
    1. Children's atlases.   [1. Atlases.] I.Title II. Title: Rand McNally discovery atlas of the world.
G1021.R165   1993 <G&M>
912--dc20   93-12560
                                 CIP
                                 MAP AC

Contents

Using the Atlas

An atlas is a book of maps. This world atlas has a few different kinds of maps. Each is especially suited for a certain topic.

The terrain maps in this atlas reveal such features as mountains and plains. They go along with the section on the terrain of each continent. These maps include oceans, lakes, rivers, glaciers, mountains, and other natural parts of the world. On the terrain map of North America, the colors and shading mean that the West has high mountains, the central part is a flat grassland, north of the Great Lakes is forested, and much of central Mexico is desert.

The maps with pictures on them—or thematic maps—show what animals live in a region and what people who live there do for a living. They go with the sections on animals and life on the land. On the picture map of the animals of North America, you can see that raccoons live around the Great Lakes.

Other maps display the world's nations and cities, roads, and railways. These are called political maps, and they go with the sections about countries and cities. They show the boundaries of each country on the continent as well as the major cities. On the political map of North America, for instance, thick gray lines represent the boundaries of countries.

Thinner gray lines show the borders between states or provinces. The thinnest gray lines reveal the locations of railroad tracks; red lines show the major roadways. Other countries, such as Canada and Mexico, are shaded with different colors.

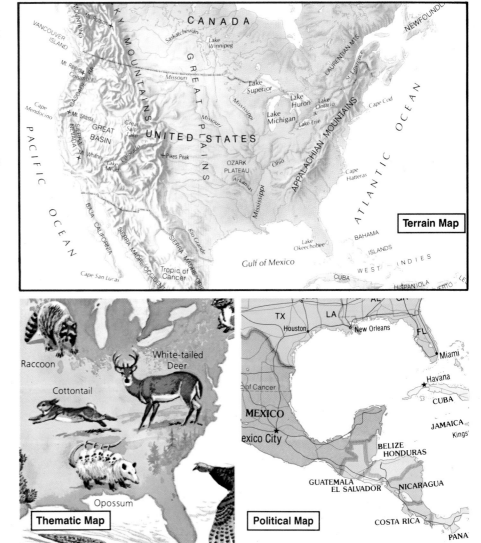

Terrain Map

Thematic Map

Political Map

Our Planet Earth

Types of Terrain

- Ice and Snow
- Grassland
- Broadleaf Trees
- Tundra and Alpine
- Desert
- Needleleaf Trees
- High Barren Area
- Dry Scrub
- Tropical Rainforest

A World of Terrain

This map shows different types of land, or terrain, that can be found on the earth. The colors and shading show the terrain, and the key to the left of the map explains what the colors mean.

The earth's surface is a wrinkled layer of solid rock called the crust. The world's oceans fill the crust's deepest basins, taking up about two-thirds of the surface. Humans occupy the highest areas on the planet—the continents of Africa, North and South America, Asia, Oceania, Europe, and bar-ren, ice-covered Antarctica.

The earth's surface constantly changes. The crust is cracked into fragments that float on a sea of liquid rock far below. Columns of this molten rock slowly rise and fall within the earth, nudging the plates that float on the

surface. As the plates of rock move, they push into their neighbors.

Sometimes two plates may lock together as they grind past each other. Pressure builds in the rock over many years. Then suddenly the rock shatters and the plates slip. This movement creates earthquakes. Volcanoes rumble to life when liquid rock from the interior of the earth finds its way to the surface.

Over millions of years, the pushing and grinding of the plates has crumpled, folded, and lifted the earth's surface. This is how mountain ranges are formed. On this map, you can easily see where the earth's mountains are. Trace the ridge of the Rockies along the western coast of North America, and the Andes along South America's west coast. Look for the Himalayas north of India.

Our Planet Earth

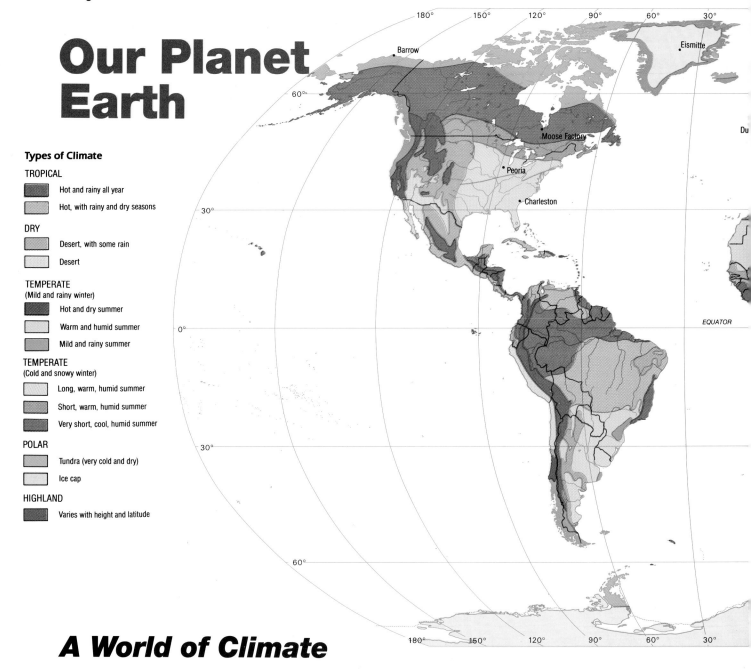

Types of Climate

TROPICAL

Hot and rainy all year

Hot, with rainy and dry seasons

DRY

Desert, with some rain

Desert

TEMPERATE
(Mild and rainy winter)

Hot and dry summer

Warm and humid summer

Mild and rainy summer

TEMPERATE
(Cold and snowy winter)

Long, warm, humid summer

Short, warm, humid summer

Very short, cool, humid summer

POLAR

Tundra (very cold and dry)

Ice cap

HIGHLAND

Varies with height and latitude

A World of Climate

This map shows different types of climate that can be found on the earth. The colors show the climates, and the key to the left of the map explains what the colors mean.

Climate and weather are not the same thing. Weather describes the temperature and rain, snow, or other moisture of an area during a short time. Climate, on the other hand, describes the same things but for a much longer period of time. It takes many years to determine a region's climate.

Climates around the world vary for different reasons. In general, the world's climates are hotter closer to the equator and colder as you go farther north or south. Climates can be affected by large bodies of water, ocean currents, and by the terrain.

Water in oceans and other large bodies stores heat, both warming up and cooling off slower than

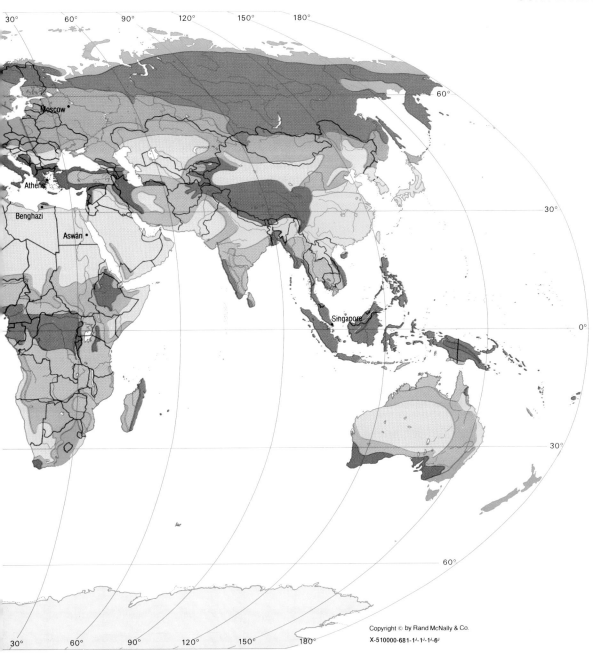

land. In daily weather, days tend to be somewhat cooler along the seacoasts than in areas farther inland, and nights tend to be slightly warmer. Over the year, summers and winters tend to be milder along coasts. Ocean currents can also have an important influence on climate.

Water evaporates from the oceans, rises, cools, forms droplets, and falls as rain onto the land. Usually, regions of heaviest rainfall are along the equator. The reddish areas on the map show the great rain forests of the world.

Terrain can have a major effect on precipi-tation. Mountain ranges force moist air to rise over them, often creating heavy rains on one side of the range—and very little on the other.

Our Planet Earth

Major Activities

- Manufacturing and trade
- Farming: Raising crops and animals
- Raising animals on rangeland
- Tropical hunting, fishing, food collecting, and primitive farming
- Nomadic animal herding (deserts)
- Forestry; lumber and pulpwood with some hunting and fishing
- Sub-arctic hunting, fishing, food collecting with some forestry
- Animal herding, hunting and fishing
- Important fishing regions
- Little or no economic activity

A World of Activity

This map shows different types of human activities. What people do for a living, or the way that they earn money, is called an economic activity. The colors show what many people in the region do for a living, and the key to the left of the map explains what the colors mean.

The character of the land has much to do with its use. The farmed areas shown on the map are among the most fertile on earth. The fertile plains of Europe, southeastern Asia, and central North America feed much of the world.

Very few regions of the world are used for manufacturing and trade. Many of them grew up near transportation routes.

Compare this map to the terrain map. You can often tell what the people in an area of the world do by knowing what the land is

like. For example, there is usually a lot of fishing along coastlines. Some of the world's most productive fishing areas include the coasts of North America, Europe, and the eastern coast of Asia. But sometimes you cannot predict what people do by the land on which they live. For example, people may live on good farmland, but they may not be able to farm it.

There are regions with little or no economic activity. Very often in these areas, the climate is either too cold and icy or too hot and dry. Look at Antarctica, and then look at the middle of the Sahara Desert in northern Africa. Compare this map to a climate map, and you will see why there is no economic activity in these areas.

Our Planet Earth

Population Density
Per square mile

- Uninhabited
- Under 2 inhabitants
- 2-25 inhabitants
- 25-60 inhabitants
- 60-125 inhabitants
- 125-250 inhabitants
- Over 250 inhabitants
- • Metropolitan areas over 2,000,000 population
- ◦ Metropolitan areas 1,000,000 to 2,000,000 population

A World of People

This map shows where people live. Different colors tell you how many people are found in that area of the world. The key tells you what the colors mean in terms of population density. This is a measure of the number of people living in each square mile (2.59 square kilometers) of land.

Population densities vary for many reasons, including climate and terrain. For example, the continent of Antarctica—the coldest region on Earth—is uninhabited, meaning that no one lives there permanently. The harsh climate makes settlement nearly impossible.

Lands with good climates and terrains tend to be densely populated, especially if they are good for farming. Look for the red and purple regions—the world's most thickly

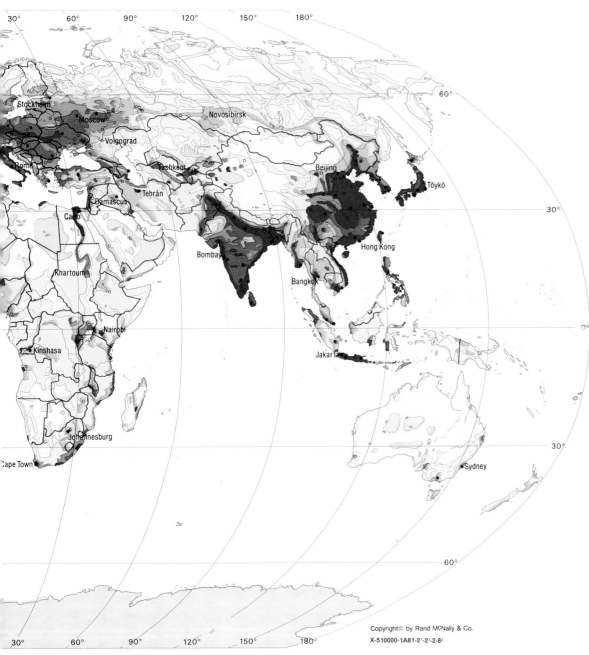

populated areas. The huge populations of India and China mostly live in the regions' rich farmlands.

In Europe and the United States, the most populous areas—the cities, or urban areas—grew up near farmland, resources, and trade routes, especially waterways. In the United States, the population is concentrated along the northeastern coast, the shores of the Great Lakes, and the banks of the Mississippi, and along the West Coast. Cities hold the greatest part of the population of Australia, Argentina, Canada, France, Japan, and the United States.

One of the world's most densely populated nations is Japan. This country is slightly smaller than the state of California but holds a population of over 123 million people.

Our Planet Earth

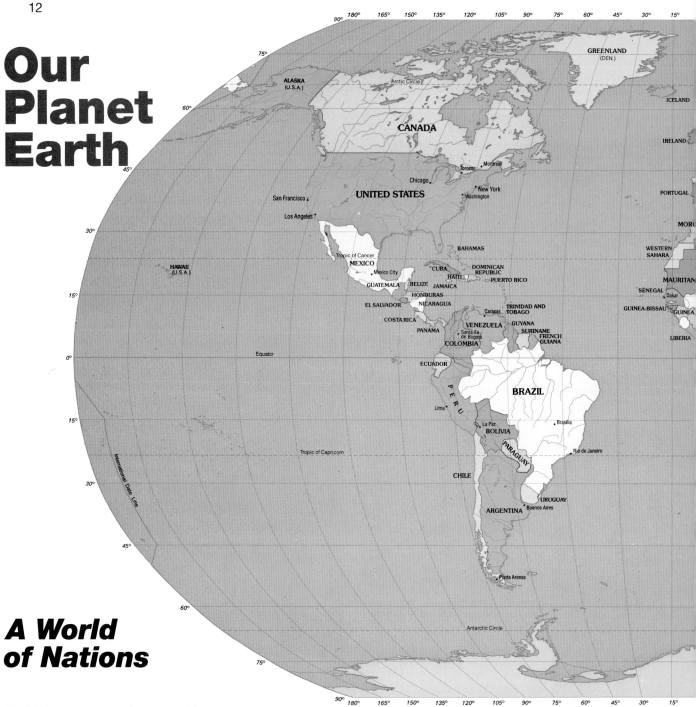

A World of Nations

This map shows the countries of the earth. The colors simply make it easier to see each separate country on the map. They do not tell you anything about each nation.

National borders are represented on the map as thin red lines. These lines divide the world into separate countries. Sometimes they follow natural formations such as mountain ranges or rivers. For example, the crooked northwestern border of China runs along a river. In some cases, though, the line is drawn by humans—as with the straight portion of the border between Canada and the United States.

Some countries are large, and some countries are small. Russia and Canada are huge nations. The world's smallest independent state is Vatican City, in Rome, Italy.

When people study the world, they often organize all the countries by land areas called continents. The seven continents are the great land divisions of the earth. Nearly all of them are large and almost completely surrounded by water.

This atlas divides the world into the seven continents: Europe, Asia, Africa, North America, South America, Antarctica, and the area in the South Pacific called Oceania. The islands of the South Pacific are grouped with Australia to form Oceania, but they are not actually part of Australia.

For each continent except Antarctica, there is a section on its terrain, or land areas; a discussion of its wild animals; a section about what the people who live there do for a living; and an overview of its countries and cities.

Europe *Terrain*

Europe

Sixth largest continent

•

Second in population: 695,200,000

•

68 cities with over 1 million population

•

Highest mountain: Elbrus, 18,510 feet (5,642 meters)

•

Rome and Chicago are the same latitude

Many parts of Europe lie in the shadows of mountains. The Alps wind through Switzerland, southeastern France, Austria, southern Germany, northern Italy, and eastward into Slovenia. Three other mountain ranges spread out from the Alps into other countries.

Across the English Channel from mainland Europe are the islands that form the United Kingdom. England lies on the biggest island, and central mountains called the Pennines run through that country.

Northern Europe has many mountains. Long ago

© 1992 Rand McNally & Co.

huge rivers of ice called glaciers ground their way across Norway and Sweden, carving deep grooves in between the mountains. The grooves flooded with water from the sea and have become long waterways called fjords. Far to the east the Ural Mountains in Russia mark the division between the continents of Europe and Asia.

Many famous rivers flow from Europe's mountains. Perhaps the best known, the Rhine, flows north out of Switzerland, past France, and through Germany and the Netherlands. The Danube is another large river that flows through Germany.

The north-central part of Europe is a fertile area known as the Great European Plain. The rich farmlands of this region supply food for much of Europe.

Many islands lie to the south of mainland Europe in the Mediterranean Sea. They include Corsica, Sardinia, Sicily, and the isles of Greece.

County Kerry, in the southwest corner of Ireland, has green pastures and rugged coastlines.

The snow-capped peaks of the Swiss Alps provide a background for these skiers.

Mykonos and the other Greek islands in the Aegean Sea are part of an ancient mountain range. The rising sea covered all but the mountain peaks.

n Sea

Europe
Animals

Skua

Herring

Barnacle Goose

Reindeer

Grey Seal

Wolverine

Lemming

Hare

Basking Shark

Red Deer

Otter

Black Grouse

Pheasant

Badger

Atlantic Salmon

Hedgehog

Rabbit

Fox

Red-legged Partridge

Stork

Marmot

Chamois

Moorhen

Squirrel

Great Bustard

Barbary Ape

Sole

Ferruginous Duck

Hoopoe

Spanish Mackerel

Raven

Whimbrel

Brown Bear

Pine Marten

Wild Boar

Wolf

Griffon Vulture

Roe Deer

Lesser Spotted Eagle

Tur

Octopus

Conger Eel

Most of the vast, animal-filled forests that once covered much of Europe were cut down long ago to make room for farms, cities, and towns. Many of Europe's animals were hunted for centuries until they were wiped out. But in the few wild places that remain, some of the animals of Europe can be found.

Wild boars can be spotted in the forests of central Europe. Wolves still live in some places. In northern Russia, the huge brown bear continues to lumber about.

Many smaller types of animals live in Europe. Foxes, badgers, moles, rabbits, and squirrels are found in many places. Lemmings abound in the mountains of Norway and Sweden. The hedgehog is common in northern Europe.

Small wildcats prowl in parts of eastern Europe. The Spanish lynx lives in Spain. The lynx is a fast, fierce hunter.

Sparrows, thrushes, finches, nightingales, and ravens are found throughout central Europe. So are large birds of prey such as falcons and eagles. During the summer, the big white stork is a common sight in cities of the Netherlands, Belgium, and Germany, where it nests on chimneys.

In a forest in Poland about 1,600 wisents, bison of prehistoric Europe, feed in grassy clearings just as they did thousands of years ago.

Europe
Life on the Land

Fishing

Hydrothermal Plant

Reindeer Herding

Coal Mining

Lumbering

Fishing

Agricultural Area

Fishing

Canneries

Papermaking

Dairyland

Fishing

Offshore Oil Drilling

Cheese Making

Dairyland

Troika (3-horse Sleigh)

Agricultural Area

Agricultural Area

Heavy Industry

Heavy Industry (Steel)

Farming

Houses of Parliament

Eiffel Tower

Bulb Farming

Grimm's Fairy Tale Country

Oil Field

Dairyland

Vineyards

Citrus Groves

Export by Sea

Matterhorn

Light Industry

Wheatlands

Sheep Raised

Cork Harvesting

Olive Orchards

Bullfighting

Water Sports

Roman Ruins

Opera

Olive Orchards

Vineyards

Fishing

Vineyards

Ancient Greek Ruins

Fur Trapping

Lumbering

Sawmills

Oil Fields

Lumbering

Oil Fields

Ballet

St. Basil's

Wheatlands

Agricultural Area

Coal Mining

Agricultural Area

Smelting of Ore

Fishing

Oil Fields

Caviar Exported

Agricultural Area

Fishing

Cotton

The whole continent of Europe juts off of Asia and into the sea. Water is everywhere. No part of western Europe is more than three hundred miles from the sea. It is no wonder that many Europeans depend on fishing or sailing to make their living.

More than half of the land of Europe is used for farming. Vineyards cover many of the hilly areas of France, Germany, Spain, and Italy. Most of the world's olives are grown in Spain, Italy, and Greece. On the flatter lands of Europe, farmers grow barley, oats, potatoes, rye, sugar beets, and wheat.

The raising of livestock is also important throughout Europe. Many farmers raise cattle, hogs, sheep, and poultry for meat. Dairy farming is especially important in Denmark, the United Kingdom, and the Netherlands.

Many world industrial leaders are European nations, including Germany, France, Great Britain, Italy, and Poland.

Europe
Countries and Cities

Usually, the borders of countries form around natural barriers, such as rivers, seas, or mountain ranges. The reason for this is these are places where people can easily defend themselves from attack. Many European nations are edged by such natural borders.

In recent years, the borders of some nations changed. When the nation called the Soviet Union broke apart in 1991, such nations as Russia, Belarus, and Ukraine became independent. The nations of Croatia and Slovakia are two of the newer independent European nations.

Today, most European countries elect their leaders. In some countries, the descendants of the kings and queens that ruled most European countries in earlier times are still treated as royalty, but they do not rule the country.

Travelers to Europe must deal with the continent's many languages. The French, Italians, Spanish, Portuguese, and Romanians speak languages that are based on ancient Latin. The people of Germany, the Netherlands, England, Denmark, Sweden, and Norway speak languages based on the German of the tribes that occupied those areas long ago. To the east, the peoples of Poland, the Czech Republic, Slovakia, Bulgaria, and other eastern European nations speak languages that are related to one another.

Europe has many big cities that are rich in history and culture. Rome, Italy, and Athens, Greece, were known thousands of years ago. Paris, France, dates back more than two thousand years. Moscow, Russia, and London, England, are Europe's two largest cities.

The large population of Paris and its surrounding area make it one of the largest cities in Europe. The Eiffel Tower in Paris is shown here.

Asia *Terrain*

Asia

Largest continent
•
First in population: 3,331,500,000
•
123 cities with over 1 million population
•
World's highest mountain: Everest, 29,028 feet (8,848 meters)
•
World's largest "lake": Caspian Sea, 143,240 square miles (370,990 square kilometers)
•
World's lowest inland point: Dead Sea, 1,312 feet (400 meters) below sea level

Asia is the largest continent. It covers more area than North America, Europe, and Australia combined. Because it is so big, it has many different types of landscapes. It has some of the world's highest mountains, longest rivers, largest deserts, and coldest and hottest climates.

Asia begins at the Ural Mountains in Russia and extends more than three thousand miles (almost five thousand kilometers), all the way to the Pacific Ocean. This northern region is known as Siberia. It is a mostly cold and barren area that is covered with ice and snow for half of the year. Few people live here.

To the south of Siberia is an equally large, equally harsh region. This area begins in the deserts of Saudi Arabia and sweeps across central Asia through Iraq, Iran, into Turkmenistan and Kazakhstan, through parts of China, and on into the deserts of Mongolia. Because of the poor climate and soil, not many people live here, either.

The region is bounded

The erosion of limestone created this unusual cone-shaped hill in southeastern China.

In northern Pakistan, apricots grown in the Himalayas dry in the sun. The Himalayas are the highest mountains in the world.

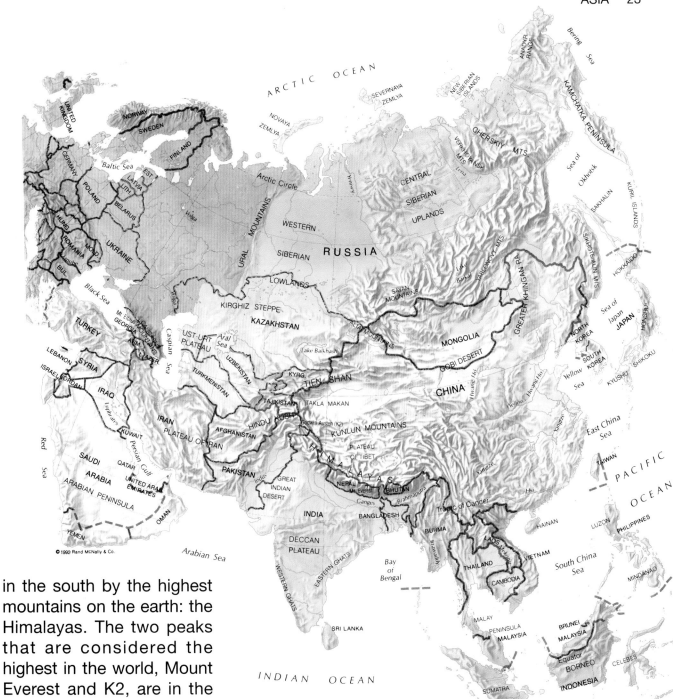

in the south by the highest mountains on the earth: the Himalayas. The two peaks that are considered the highest in the world, Mount Everest and K2, are in the Himalayas.

South of the Himalayas is a warm, wet triangle of land that contains India, Pakistan, Bangladesh, and a couple of smaller nations. Here the climate is friendlier and the land more fertile, so many people live in this area. In fact, this is one of the world's most crowded regions.

To the east lies Southeast Asia, a land that is a giant rain forest. It is very fertile and has plenty of rainfall. These factors make Southeast Asia a good place to live, so the countries of this region are highly populated.

North of Southeast Asia is an area known as the Far East. It includes most of China, North Korea, South Korea, and Japan. Many people live in these countries. In fact, China holds more people—over one billion—than any other country in the world.

Asia *Animals*

In the north, Asia is a land covered with snow nine months a year. Southern Asia is a land of steamy, hot rain forests. In between, there are deserts and mountains. Asia has a great variety of landscapes and a great variety of animals.

Large white polar bears live in the icy northernmost places. Reindeer, foxes, hare, and tiny, mouselike lemmings live in northern Asia. In northern China and Korea lives the thick-furred Siberian tiger, the biggest of all cats.

The two-humped Bactrian camel strides across the cold deserts of central Asia. Yaks—huge wild cattle covered with long, thick fur—live in the high, cold land of Tibet, in China. Camels and yaks are tamed by people and used as beasts of burden.

The forests of southern Asia swarm with animals— monkeys, leopards, wild cattle called gaurs, and an ever-dwindling number of tigers. Indian elephants move through the forests. Smaller than African elephants, they are easily tamed, and many have been trained to work for people.

In the high bamboo forests in part of central China lives the giant panda. Mostly white with black legs, ears, and eye patches, this gentle bear-like creature is active mostly at night. The smaller red panda, which looks some-thing like a raccoon, can be found in the Himalayas and the mountains of western China and northern Burma (Myanmar).

Imperial Eagle

Jackal

Dromedary

Jerbo

Ibex

The largest horns grown by any animal are those of a sheep called the Pamir argali, or Marco Polo's argali. Marco Polo found this unusual creature during his travels across central Asia.

Polar Bear

Killer Whale

Arctic Fox

Willow Grouse

Sea Eagle

Elk

Snowy Owl

Wolf

Harbor Seal

Lynx

Przewalski's Horse

Raccoon-like Dog

Japanese Macaque

Saiga

Yak

Giant Panda

Bactrian Camel

Mandarin Duck

Japanese Crane

Snow Leopard

Pheasant

Water Buffalo

Dolphin

Indian Elephant

Cormorant

Flyingfish

Tiger

Peafowl

Gibbon

Cobra

Orangutan

Macaque

Mongoose

Asia
Life on the Land

More than half the earth's people live on the vast continent of Asia. Throughout the world, people naturally tend to live in areas where the climate and land are good for producing food. About two-thirds of Asia's population make their living by farming, and the continent's farming areas are among its most crowded.

In much of China, Japan, India, and Southeast Asia, the most important crop is rice. It is the main food of many Asian people, and Asia produces most of the world's rice.

Cotton is the main crop of parts of southwestern Asia, also known as the Middle East.

The land of northern Asia is too cold for much farming, and the soil in central Asia is not good for growing crops. In these regions, some people raise reindeer, cattle, and sheep.

Petroleum, or crude oil, is a precious substance in today's world. Beneath the deserts of the Middle East lie some of the world's greatest oil reserves. The countries of this region sell oil to many other countries around the world.

In the Middle East, people tell a story about a young boy named Aladdin, who finds an old lamp. When he rubs the lamp, a genie appears and grants him three wishes.

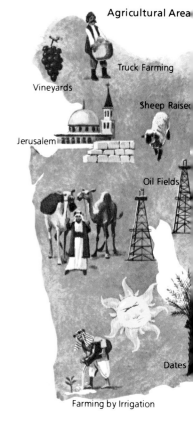

Agricultural Area

Truck Farming

Vineyards

Sheep Raised

Jerusalem

Oil Fields

Dates

Farming by Irrigation

The Indonesian island of Bali, off of Southeast Asia, is known for its folk dances. One tells an ancient story of love and war.

Mining

Fur Trapping

Logging

Truck Farming

Reindeer Herds

Mining

Smelting of Ore

Mining

Truck Farming

Logging

Rice Grown

Cossack Dancer

Mining

Light and Heavy Industry

Wheatlands

Wheatlands

Tea Grown

Great Wall of China

Steel Manufactured

Hydroelectric Power

Gate of Heavenly Peace

Citrus Fruits Grown

Sheep Raised

Farming

Chinese Junk

Smelting of Ore

Goods Shipped by Caravan

Traditional Chinese Urn

Agricultural Area

Ruins of Persepolis, Persia

Palace of the Dalai Lama

Agricultural Area

Persian Carpet

Corn

Manufacturing

Cacao (Chocolate)

Cotton

Wheat

Mt. Everest

Bathing in the Sacred Ganges

Coconuts

Taj Mahal

Fishing

Burmese Temples

Logging

Rice Grown

Tea Grown

Oil

Coconuts

Fishing

Agricultural Area

Rubber

Teak

Coffee

Asia
Countries and Cities

Asia has five large groupings of nations. The first, which borders the eastern edge of the continent, is called the Far East. Its leading countries include China and Japan. China holds the most people of any nation—over one billion. One out of every five persons on earth is Chinese. But in terms of business, Japan is a giant. The tiny island nation is one of the world's leading industrial powers.

Southeast Asia and the islands of Indonesia make up the second group. Many of the nations here formed around river valleys where food grows well.

With a history of more than five thousand years, Jerusalem, Israel, has long been a holy city of Christianity, Judaism, and Islam.

© 1992 Rand McNally & Co.

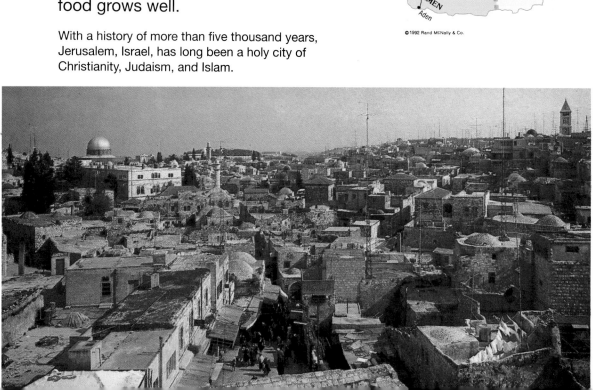

Roads
Railroads

The third group formed within the triangle of land that contains India, Pakistan, Bangladesh, and Sri Lanka. The number of people living in India is second only to China. These nations struggle with poverty.

The desert countries make up a fourth cluster. Fewer people live here. Only in Israel does the population density approach that of European countries.

Siberia, a part of northern Russia, stands alone as the fifth. Its people are few and far between.

Some of the largest cities in the world are in Asia. Tokyo, Japan, has more people than any other city in the world. Osaka is another very large Japanese city, and Seoul, South Korea is also huge. China and India both have several very big cities.

Africa
Terrain

Africa

Second largest continent
•
Third in population: 694,000,000
•
26 cities with over 1 million population
•
Highest mountain: Kilimanjaro,
19,340 feet (5,895 meters)
•
World's largest desert: Sahara,
approximately 3,500,000 square miles
(9,065,000 square kilometers)
•
World's longest river system: Nile,
4,145 miles (6,671 kilometers)
•
World's highest recorded temperature:
Azizia, Libya, 136.4°F (58°C)
•
Equator passes through

The continent of Africa is second in size only to Asia. Few people realize just how huge it is. For comparison, the United States is about the size of the Sahara Desert in northern Africa.

Many people imagine Africa as a land of rain forests. In reality, most of Africa is covered with desert or grassland. The Sahara takes up most of northern Africa. The Kalahari and Namib deserts lie in the south. Between these two desert regions are many, many miles of grassland called savanna. Rain forests are found in the middle of the continent.

The mountains of Africa include the Atlas Mountains that arch across the top of the continent. The Drakensberg Mountains are found in southern Africa. In East Africa is snow-capped

Shown here is the savanna that covers much of Africa. This particular savanna is in the nation of Zambia.

Africa's Great Rift Valley extends about four thousand miles (almost 6,500 kilometers). It can be traced along the many lakes and seas that fill parts of it.

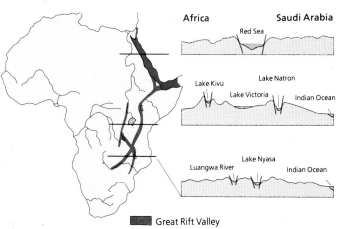

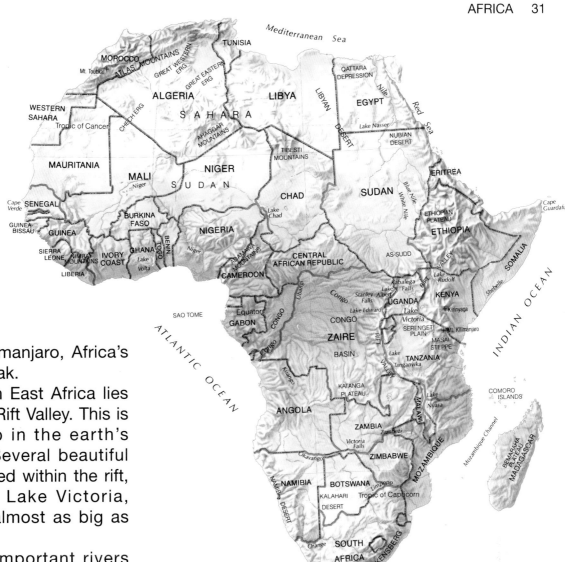

Mount Kilimanjaro, Africa's highest peak.

Also in East Africa lies the Great Rift Valley. This is a long rip in the earth's surface. Several beautiful lakes pooled within the rift, including Lake Victoria, which is almost as big as Scotland.

Four important rivers flow out of Africa. The Niger runs through West Africa and out into the Atlantic Ocean. The Congo flows west out of central Africa. The Zambezi, toward southern Africa, flows east to the Indian Ocean. And finally, the great Nile flows northward through several countries, including Egypt, and empties into the Mediterranean Sea. The Nile is the longest river in the world.

Palm trees line the shore along the Gulf of Guinea, which lies to the south of Ghana.

Africa *Animals*

Africa is a continent of rain forests, grassy plains, and deserts. Each different type of land has different types of animals. Many of the animals of Africa are in danger of becoming extinct, as people hunt them and use their lands for towns and farms.

In the north, the huge Sahara Desert spreads across thousands of miles. Not many animals can live here. Those that do are able to survive with little or no water. The best-known animal of the Sahara is the one-humped Arabian camel.

Great rain forests are found in central Africa. Chimpanzees and gorillas live here, feeding on fruit and other plants. Both are very smart creatures. Here, too, are found buffalo, leopards, and many kinds of monkeys. In the swamps and rivers of the forest the crocodile swims and the hippopotamus munches on water plants.

The vast, grassy plains that lie north and south of the central rain forests contain many of the continent's best-known animals. Herds of zebra and wildebeest graze on the plains. Giraffes graze among small groups of trees. Rhinoceroses lounge in the mud after feeding. Herds of African elephants, the largest of all land animals, rumble across the plains, or savanna. The spotted cheetah, fastest of all animals, prowls the grasslands in search of prey. It must compete with an even more famous cat, however, for the African lion also hunts on the African plains.

Tarpon
Addax
Fennec
Pangolin
Colobus Monkey

Gorillas are gentle beasts who eat plants. Like many African animals, gorillas are in danger. They are hunted, and their forest home is being cut down.

Jackal
Dromedary
Crowned Crane
Eared Vulture
Dorcas Gazelle
Barbary Sheep
Crocodile
Striped Hyena
Greater Kudu
Aardvark
Elephant
Giraffe
Baboon
Chimpanzee
Gorilla
Black Rhinoceros
Leopard
Hornbill
White Pelican
Cape Buffalo
Hippopotamus
Zebra
Lion
Tenrec
Eland
Chameleon
Python
Wildebeest
Ring-tailed Lemur
Cheetah
Angelfish
Impala
Ostrich
Sacred Ibis

Africa

Life on the Land

Some Africans carve masks by hand, as they have for centuries. This mask is too big to wear and is used as a decoration.

Agricultural Area

Peanuts

Chocolate

Little farming can be done in hot, dry North Africa. But along the coasts of Morocco, Algeria, and Tunisia, farmers can grow a few crops. About half the people of Egypt work farms along the banks of the Nile, mainly growing cotton.

Drilling for oil is important to several African countries. There are oil fields in Algeria and Libya in the north and in Nigeria and Gabon farther south.

West Africa is an important agricultural area. Among other crops, people here grow cacao beans, from which chocolate and cocoa are made. The forests of central Africa pro-duce rubber trees and banana trees. In East Africa, herding cattle has been the main way of life for many years.

The Kalahari Desert covers thousands of square miles of southern Africa, mostly within the country of Botswana. The Kalahari is the home of the Bushmen, who hunt and gather whatever food they can find.

Farther south, in the country of South Africa, the fertile land is farmed by the descendants of Europeans who settled there many years ago. Most of the world's diamonds and much of its gold come from South African mines.

Ananse the Spider Man is a character in a famous African tale. Ananse gathered all the wisdom in the world into a huge pot and tried to keep it for himself. But the pot fell as Ananse tried to hide it in a tree, and all the wisdom blew away.

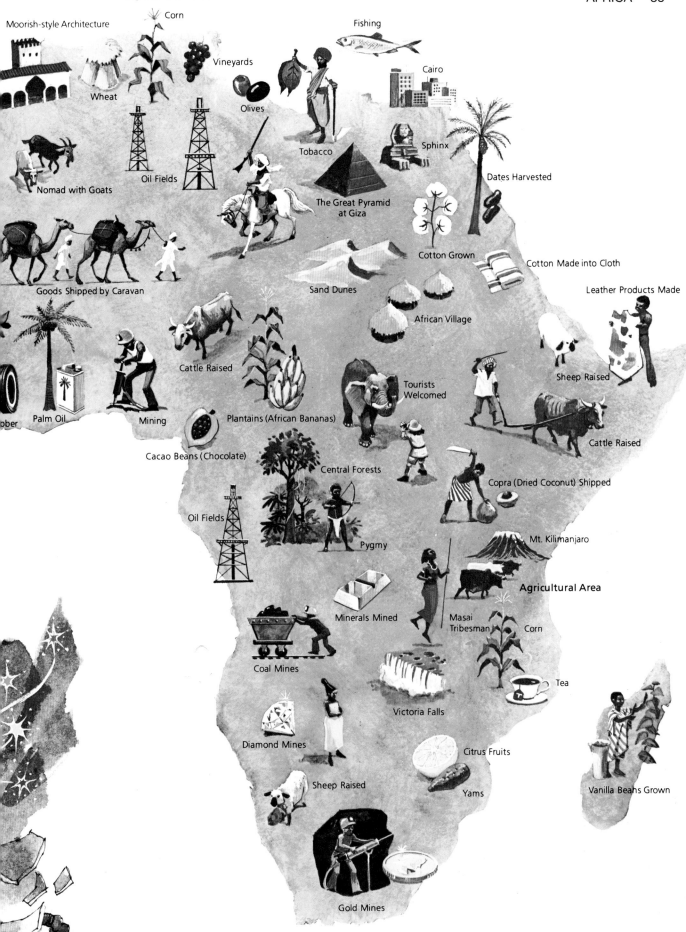

Agricultural Area

Moorish-style Architecture

Corn

Wheat

Vineyards

Olives

Fishing

Cairo

Sphinx

Dates Harvested

Nomad with Goats

Oil Fields

Tobacco

The Great Pyramid at Giza

Cotton Grown

Cotton Made into Cloth

Goods Shipped by Caravan

Sand Dunes

African Village

Leather Products Made

Palm Oil

Mining

Cattle Raised

Plantains (African Bananas)

Tourists Welcomed

Sheep Raised

Cattle Raised

Cacao Beans (Chocolate)

Copra (Dried Coconut) Shipped

Oil Fields

Central Forests

Pygmy

Mt. Kilimanjaro

Minerals Mined

Masai Tribesman

Agricultural Area

Corn

Coal Mines

Victoria Falls

Tea

Diamond Mines

Citrus Fruits

Sheep Raised

Yams

Vanilla Beans Grown

Gold Mines

Africa
Countries and Cities

Human history began in Africa. Scientists believe the earliest human beings walked the grasslands of East Africa about two million years ago. Over

Roads
Railroads

Algiers · Tunis
Rabat · Casablanca
TUNISIA
Tripoli
MOROCCO
Alexandria
Cairo
ALGERIA
LIBYA
EGYPT
WESTERN SAHARA
Tropic of Cancer
Aswan
MAURITANIA
Nouakchott
CAPE VERDE
MALI
NIGER
Dakar · SENEGAL
GAMBIA
Bamako
CHAD
Khartoum
ERITREA
Asmera
GUINEA-BISSAU
Niamey
BURKINA FASO
SUDAN
DJIBOUTI
GUINEA
Conakry
N'Djamena
ETHIOPIA
Addis Ababa
Freetown
SIERRA LEONE
IVORY COAST
GHANA
TOGO
BENIN
NIGERIA
CENTRAL AFRICAN REPUBLIC
LIBERIA
Abidjan
Accra
Lagos
CAMEROON
SOMALIA
Yaounde
EQUATORIAL GUINEA
SAO TOME AND PRINCIPE
Libreville
UGANDA
KENYA
Mogadishu
GABON
CONGO
Equator
Kampala
Nairobi
RWANDA
BURUNDI
Mombasa
Brazzaville
ZAIRE
CABINDA (ANG.)
Kinshasa
TANZANIA
Dar es Salaam
Luanda
COMOROS

The Masai people cross the boundary between Kenya and Tanzania often in search of water and grazing lands for their cattle.

ANGOLA
MALAWI
ZAMBIA
Lusaka
Harare
ZIMBABWE
MOZAMBIQUE
Antananari
MADAGASCAR
NAMIBIA
Windhoek
BOTSWANA
Walvis Bay (S. AFRICA)
Tropic of Capricorn
Gaborone
Pretoria
Johannesburg
SWAZ.
Maputo
LESOTHO
Durban
SOUTH AFRICA
Cape Town

The people of Tunisia live mostly along the coast. Farther inland, into the Sahara Desert, there are villages made of stone and mud.

Harare, pictured here, is the capital and largest city of Zimbabwe, in southern Africa.

many years, humans moved out from Africa to other parts of the world.

Civilization has a long history in North Africa. The Nile Valley of Egypt cradled the center of one of the world's oldest civilizations, which developed over five thousand years ago. Some of the cities of Egypt, including Alexandria and Cairo, are more than one thousand years old. Cairo is also the biggest city in Africa.

By the 1400s, Europeans began sailing to Africa and conquering the peoples who lived there. By the early 1900s, almost all of Africa was under European rule. Most of the European governments are gone now, replaced with African governments.

Today, more than one-fourth of the people in Africa live in West Africa. Nigeria, with over 110 million people, has the greatest number of people of any African country.

The equator passes through central Africa. Zaire, covered with rain forest, is the biggest country in this region.

Oceania
Australia
Smallest continent
•
Population: 17,420,000
•
Highest mountain: Kosciusko, 7,316 feet (2,230 meters)
•
New Zealand
Two main islands, North Island and South Island
•
Population: 3,463,000
•
Oceania
(not including Australia and New Zealand)
•
20,000 islands—more or less—scattered throughout the Pacific
•
Populations: 6,417,000

Deep in the heart of Australia lies a group of worn-down sandstone rocks called the Olgas. They tower above the desert landscape.

Oceania
Terrain

A map of the world shows you just how big the Pacific Ocean is. It covers more than one-third of the earth's surface. You can also see that the ocean is full of islands of different sizes. There are between twenty and thirty thousand of them. Australia, New Zealand, and other islands are in a region known as Oceania. They lie within the vast Pacific like stepping stones across a pond.

Some of the small islands of Oceania are the tips of volcanoes that have pushed their way above the water. Others are rings of coral surrounding lagoons that remain where volcanoes have sunk back into the sea.

Australia is the smallest continent. The mountains of eastern Australia are called the Great Dividing Range. East of the mountains, plenty of rain and fertile soils make this the continent's main agricultural area. West of the Great Dividing Range is the continent's great desert region. Australians call it the Outback.

The Cape York Peninsula is very different from the rest of Australia. Heat and rain combine to make ideal conditions for the tropical rain forests that grow there.

Perhaps the most famous region of Australia is not on the land, but in the ocean off the northeastern coast. It is called the Great Barrier Reef. Built from colorful coral, it is the largest coral reef in the world.

Two main islands make up New Zealand: North Island and South Island. On South Island, long, beautiful fjords cut into the land. North Island has a volcanic region where geysers blast hot water skyward and pools of mud bubble with steam.

The Isle of Pines is one of several islands that make up New Caledonia, which is ruled by France.

Oceania

Animals

Many of the animals of Australia are very different from those in other places. Two of the strangest animals are the echidna, or spiny anteater, and the duck-billed platypus. They are furry, warm-blooded animals, but their babies hatch out of eggs, like birds or reptiles.

On the plains of Australia, kangaroos live in little herds and eat grass. Some kangaroos can be quite tall, but there are also small kangaroos called wallabies. Wombats look like beavers without tails. They dig tunnels that they sleep in during the day, and then look for food at night. Ratlike, long-snouted bandicoots live much the same way as wombats.

Dingoes also roam the dry plains of Australia. A member of the dog family, the dingo has long legs, a wolflike head, and yellow-red fur. It hunts at night, preying on small animals and often on livestock. The dingo was probably brought to the continent by prehistoric settlers.

In the eastern part of Australia lives the koala. Koalas look like little bears, but in fact they are not even closely related to bears.

On some islands near New Zealand live little reptiles called tuataras. They are the last survivors of a group of reptiles that once included some dinosaurs. The kiwi is another of New Zealand's unusual animals. About the size of a chicken, this bird that does not fly has short legs and dark feathers.

Great numbers of sea creatures drift among the coral reefs and other waters surrounding the islands of Oceania. The Great Barrier Reef off Australia is well known.

Blue Angelfish

Pacific Sheepshead

Albacore

Ocean Sunfish

Eagle Ray

Imperial Angelfish

Regal Angelfish

Sea Horse

Viperfish

Opah

Black Marlin

Triggerfish

Butterfly Fish

Cockatoo

Cassowary

Dingo

Death Adder

Tree Kangaroo

Echidna

Emu

Frilled Lizard

Rabbit

Rock Wallaby

Wombat

Great Gray Kangaroo

Kookaburra

Koala

Red Kangaroo

Platypus

Wandering Albatross

White Shark

Slender-billed Shearwater

Black Swan

The koala looks like a teddy bear. For six months the koala cub rides in its mother's pouch. Later it rides on her back, even when she climbs high up trees in search of food.

Dovey Petrel

Kiwi

Tuatara

Kea

Oceania
Life on the Land

Lumbering
Rain Forest
Water Sports
Sheep Raising
Lumbering
Water Conservation
Uranium Prospecting
Great Barrier Reef
Aborigines in the Outback
Cattle Raising
Mining
Agricultural Area
Ayers Rock
Sheep Raising
Rugby
Going to School by Radio
Mining
Opals Mined
Sydney— Opera House
Lifeguard Team
Minerals Mined
Citrus Groves
Agricultural Area
Agricultural Area
Wheatlands
Water Sports
Freighter
Fishing
Fruit Grown
Minerals Exported

Maori Carving

Sheep Raising

Australia may be the smallest continent, but it is one of the largest countries. Its population clings mostly to the eastern and southeastern coasts. There are many Australian farmers who raise sheep and cattle. In New Zealand, the mild climate and excellent grazing land make the raising of sheep and cattle very important.

Years ago, many Europeans traveled to Oceania and settled among the islands. In Australia, New Zealand, and neighboring islands, there remain groups of people who were living here long before the Europeans arrived. In Australia there are people known as Aboriginals, whose ancestors may have arrived up to 40,000 years ago. The Maori of New Zealand settled in the 1100s.

Oceania
Countries and Cities

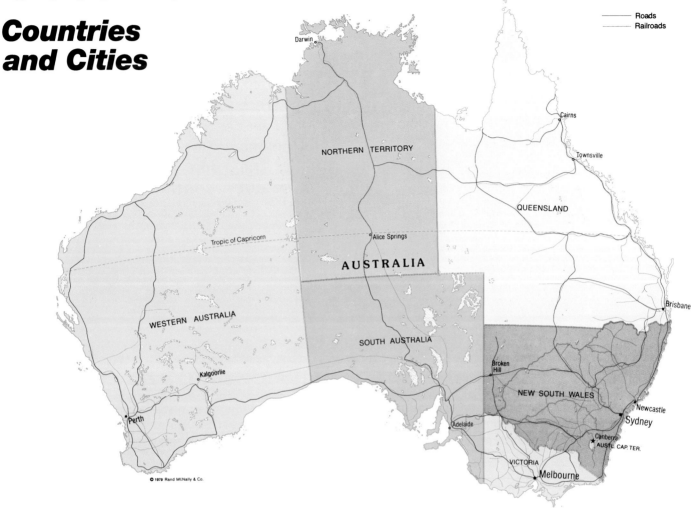

The Land Down Under—that's what Australia and New Zealand are often called. The nickname grew out of the idea that these lands are directly opposite, that is, under the feet of, Europeans. And in some ways, things in these lands behave opposite from what you'd expect in Europe. In Australia, to go north is to head for the equator, where the land is closer to the sun, and it is warmer. To go south is to travel toward cold weather. Winter occurs in July and summer in January.

The descendants of Europeans who live in Australia and New Zealand speak English. There are groups of people in these places and on the surrounding islands who have lived there since ancient times. Most of them speak English as well as the languages of their ancestors.

North America

Third largest continent

•

Fourth in population: 436,300,000

•

48 cities with over 1 million population

•

Highest mountain: McKinley, 20,320 feet (6,194 meters)

•

World's largest island: Greenland

•

Location of North Magnetic Pole

North America
Terrain

North America has many mountains. In the west, mountains stretch from Alaska at the northern end of the continent to Panama at the southern end. The Rocky Mountains rise out of the Great Plains and reach way up into Canada.

Many other mountain ranges rise west of the Rockies. Some of them, like the Cascade Range, contain volcanoes. The

Coral reefs and underwater volcanoes formed the islands of the Caribbean. Shown here is a small, volcanic island named Saba.

The Canadian province of British Columbia is the site of several national parks, including Yoho National Park, shown here.

Monument Valley lies on the border between Utah and Arizona. Here sandstone buttes, mesas, and arches rise above the sandy plain below.

Great Basin lies between the western mountain chains. It is a desert region. Farther south, another desert region covers much of the American Southwest and reaches deep into Mexico.

Central America, at the south end of North America, is mainly mountainous. There are many volcanoes here. The small country of Guatemala alone has more than thirty of them.

The mountains of eastern North America are much lower than the ones to the west. One such range is the Appalachians, the biggest mountain range in the eastern United States.

The Great Plains lie at the center of North America. Here the land is mostly flat or gently rolling as far as the eye can see. The land is also very fertile, and many crops are grown here.

The Mississippi and Missouri rivers form the longest river system in North America. Lake Superior, one of the five Great Lakes, is the largest freshwater lake in the world. The Panama Canal, near the southern tip of North America, is a human-made strip of water that allows ships to pass between the Atlantic and the Pacific oceans without having to go all the way around the southern tip of South America.

North America

Animals

As the number of people in North America has increased, the number of wild animals has decreased. The American bison and the pronghorn antelope were once nearly wiped out by hunters. Today they are found in protected areas on the Great Plains.

Wolves and grizzly bears prowl in the north. The bald eagle, the national bird of the United States, is still found in the Northwest.

The coyote preys on prairie dogs, mice, rabbits, and sometimes on livestock or pets. The raccoon can be found in many places from southern Canada to South America. Looking like a masked bandit, it forages at night and will feed on garbage. Both animals seem to thrive near people.

Many kinds of rattlesnakes, named for the rattles on their tails, inhabit North America. The coral snake lives in the deserts, as does a poisonous lizard called the Gila monster.

In the swamps and rivers of the southeastern part of the continent lives the alligator. These meat-eating reptiles are hunted for their skins, but they are now protected by law.

Sea otters and sea lions frolic in the ocean off the West Coast. So do some of the biggest of all animals—California gray whales.

Experts say that most of the animals that have ever lived on earth are now extinct. This drawing shows some extinct animals and how long ago they became extinct.

Apatosaurus
135 Million Years Ago

Tyrannosaurus
70 Million Years Ago

Woolly Mammoth
10 Thousand Years Ago

Great Auk
Mid Nineteenth Century

Saber-Toothed Cat
1 Million Years Ago

Passenger Pigeon
Late Nineteenth Century

Grizzly Bear

Walrus

Herring Gull

Canada Goose

Polar Bear

Mountain Goat

Red Fox

Gray Wolf

Rock Ptarmigan

Beaver

Porcupine

Bald Eagle

Mountain Lion

Moose

Robin

Gray Squirrel

King Salmon

Elk

Pronghorn

Raccoon

White-tailed Deer

Willet

Sea Otter

Bison

Cottontail

Gambel's Quail

Diamondback Rattlesnake

Opossum

Turkey

Peccary

Alligator

California Sea Lions

Armadillo

Roseate Spoonbill

Brown Pelican

Squirrel Monkey

Gray Whale

North America *Life on the Land*

Ice hockey is a popular sport played by both amateurs and professionals in Canada and the United States.

The United States and Canada are the two largest countries in North America. They are also among the richest nations in the world.

North America has much fertile farmland and a good climate for growing a variety of crops. Both the United States and Canada grow far more than their people eat, so they sell food to other countries. Farming is done with modern methods and machinery. This means that fewer farmers can grow more crops. For this reason, not many people are farmers in the United States and Canada.

North America's rich forests and mineral reserves have helped the United States and Canada to become world leaders in manufacturing. Many cities in these countries have been huge industrial centers for many years.

Agriculture is very important in Mexico and in other countries of North America as well. Corn is grown in Mexico. In Central America and the islands in the Caribbean, coffee, sugarcane, and bananas are grown. The warm, sunny climates of Mexico, Central America, and the Caribbean attract many tourists.

According to folklore, the giant Paul Bunyan and his enormous blue ox Babe created much of America's landscape. The legend claims that they dug the St. Lawrence River in three weeks using a shovel as large as a house.

Greenland

Canneries

Mining

Alaskan
Pipeline

Oil Fields

Salmon Fishing
and Canning

Lumbering

Fur Trapping

Totem Pole

Fishing

Ski Trails

Lumbering

Canadian Wheatlands

Giant Redwoods

Agricultural Area

Wheat

Potatoes

Dairyland

Mt. Rushmore

Statue of Liberty

Offshore Oil Drilling

Truck Farming

Hollywood

Soybeans

Agricultural Area

Cars
Manufactured

Washington, D.C.

Citrus Groves

Agricultural Area

Longhorn Cattle

Corn

Peanuts

Tobacco

Corn

Cotton

Citrus Groves

Cape Canaveral

Sugarcane

Olmec Sculpture

Oil Fields

Ruins of Ancient Pyramids

Agricultural Area

Sugarcane Made
into Molasses

A famous ballet group in
Mexico performs many
dances. The dancers here
wear costumes modeled after
those worn by the Mayas, an
Indian people who lived in
Mexico a thousand years ago.

Coffee

Bananas

North America

Countries and cities

Mexico City is the capital and fastest-growing city of that nation. After Tokyo, Japan, it is the second largest city in the world.

Most of North America is divided among three nations: Canada, the United States, and Mexico. The United States is the giant of North America in population. It has more than twice the people of Canada and Mexico combined.

Central America is considered part of North America. It covers an area less than a third the size of Mexico and contains seven countries. Many of the islands of the Caribbean are independent nations, but some of them are governed by larger countries, such as the United States.

Native Americans were the first people to live in North America. The Europeans who began coming to North America around the year 1500 conquered the American Indians. The countries of North America are now mainly made up of descendants of Europeans, as well as many African Americans and other groups. Most North Americans live in nations where the leaders are elected by the people.

The main language of each North American nation is the language spoken in the European country that once ruled the area.

For example, Spain once ruled Mexico, and although Mexico rules itself now, its people still speak Spanish. Most people in Canada and

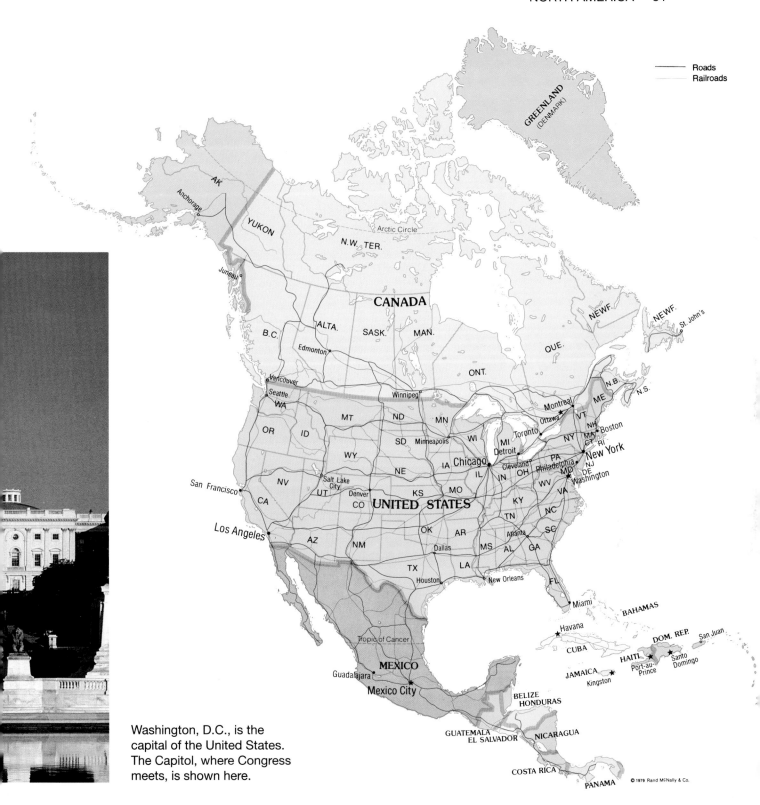

Roads
Railroads

GREENLAND
(DENMARK)

AK
Anchorage
YUKON
Arctic Circle
Juneau
N.W. TER.
CANADA
NEWF.
NEWF.
St. John's
B.C.
ALTA.
SASK.
MAN.
QUE.
Edmonton
ONT.
N.B.
N.S.
Vancouver
Seattle
Winnipeg
Montreal
ME
WA
Ottawa
VT
NH
Boston
MT
ND
MN
Toronto
NY
MA
OR
ID
WI
MI
CT RI
SD
Minneapolis
Detroit
New York
WY
IA
Chicago
Cleveland
PA
NJ
San Francisco
NV
Salt Lake
City
NE
IL
IN
OH
Philadelphia
MD
DE
Washington
UT
Denver
KS
MO
WV
VA
CA
CO
UNITED STATES
KY
NC
Los Angeles
TN
AZ
NM
OK
AR
Atlanta
SC
Dallas
MS
AL
GA
TX
LA
Houston
New Orleans
FL
Miami
BAHAMAS
Havana
Tropic of Cancer
CUBA
DOM. REP.
San Juan
HAITI
Santo
Domingo
JAMAICA
Port-au-
Prince
MEXICO
Kingston
Guadalajara
Mexico City
BELIZE
HONDURAS
GUATEMALA
NICARAGUA
EL SALVADOR
COSTA RICA
PANAMA
© 1979 Rand McNally & Co.

Washington, D.C., is the
capital of the United States.
The Capitol, where Congress
meets, is shown here.

the United States speak
English.

Cities tend to grow up
around areas that are trade
routes. For example, Chi-
cago, Illinois, grew up on a
crossroads that linked the
Great Lakes and the Mis-
sissippi River. Today, some
of the world's biggest and
most modern cities are in
North America. Mexico City
and New York City are two
of the largest cities in the
world.

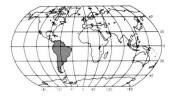

South America

Fourth largest continent

•

Fifth in population: 306,700,000

•

30 cities with over 1 million population

•

Highest mountain: Aconcagua,
22,831 feet (6,959 meters)

•

World's highest waterfall: Angel Falls,
3,212 feet (979 meters)

•

Equator passes through

Between the high, snow-capped peaks of the Andes, good farmland can be found. This scene is in the Andes of Peru.

South America
Terrain

Wind and water have molded the sandstone and shale of this part of Guyana into a variety of interesting formations.

The Andes Mountains run down the entire western side of South America. The Andes chain is the longest in the world. This range also has some of the world's tallest peaks. Only the Himalayas in Asia are higher. There are several smaller mountain ranges in South America.

Where Argentina, Bolivia, and Chile meet, the Andes split into two ranges. Between them is a high, flat area, and Lake Titicaca.

In northern Chile, between the Andes and the Pacific, is the Atacama Desert. This desert is near the ocean, yet it is one of the driest spots on earth. In some parts of the Atacama, no rainfall has ever been recorded.

Many rivers and streams tumble from the Andes and other highland areas. The Amazon River begins in the Andes of Peru and flows to the Atlantic Ocean. The Amazon contains more water than any other river on earth.

The Amazon flows out of a huge plain called the Amazon River basin, an area almost as big as the United States. The equator runs through this area, so it is very warm, and it receives a lot of rainfall. These factors combine to make this region the

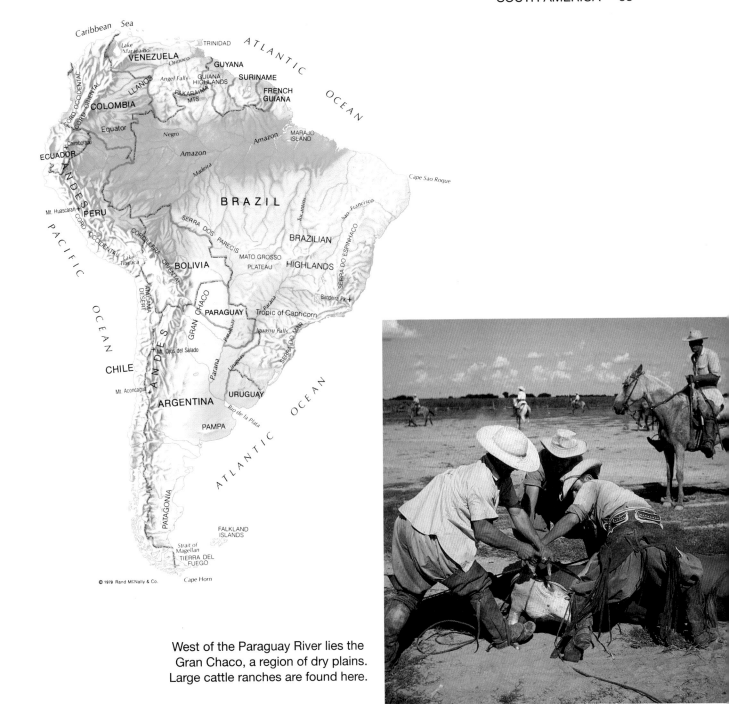

West of the Paraguay River lies the
Gran Chaco, a region of dry plains.
Large cattle ranches are found here.

biggest tropical rain forest on earth.

Another plain stretches across Paraguay and most of Argentina. It is made up of two different areas—the Gran Chaco and the Pampa. The Gran Chaco is a dry region with few trees. The Pampa receives more rain. It is a grassland that is ideal for grazing cattle and sheep. Patagonia lies near the southern tip of South America. At the very tip of South America is a group of islands called Tierra del Fuego.

South America

Animals

The Amazon rain forests provide homes for many animals. The jaguar, a big spotted cat, prowls among the trees at night. Herds of piglike peccaries root in the underbrush. The tapir, an animal that looks like a large hog with a long nose, also lives in the forest. It is related to both the horse and rhinoceros. Tapirs are also found in Southeast Asia.

The trees of the rain forest brighten with colorful parrots, macaws, toucans, and other birds. Monkeys howl and shriek from the treetops. Sloths hang upside down from the branches and feed on leaves at night. The boa constrictor and the anaconda, two very large snakes, also live in the rain forest.

On the plains of South America live giant anteaters, long-legged maned wolves, and large birds called rheas.

In the Andes live llamas, vicuñas, and alpacas. Some of these animals have been tamed by people who use them like sheep or cattle. The spectacled bear lives on mountain slopes. It gets its name from the circles of yellowish fur, like eyeglass frames, around its eyes. The chinchilla also lives in the mountain heights. It is a bushy-tailed, mouselike creature with the finest, silkiest fur in the world. Gliding through the air between the mountain peaks is the great South American condor, one of the largest flying birds in the world.

The Galápagos Islands lie off the coast of Ecuador. Here live rare cormorants that cannot fly, great lizardlike iguanas, and giant tortoises.

Sloth

Tapir

Manatee

Scarlet Ibis

Coatimundi

Ocelot

Piranha

Green Turtle

Toucan

Caiman

Spectacled Bear

Llama

Spider Monkey

Red Brocket Deer

Anaconda

Vampire Bat

Capybara

Jaguar

Howling Monkey

Macaw

Chinchilla

Vicuña

Great Anteater

Condor

Guanaco

Maned Wolf

Brazilian Lapwing

Alpaca

Pampas Deer

Blue Marlin

Torrent Duck

Rhea

Elephant Seal

Magellan Goose

Magellan Penguin

Cavy

Black-necked Swan

Sperm Whale

South America
Life on the Land

Close to half of all South Americans make their living by farming. Most farms are quite small and can produce only enough food for the families that own them. There are huge modern farms and ranches. Some of them are larger than some of the small states of the United States. Herds of sheep and beef cattle are raised on these giant ranches. Many of them are in Argentina.

Drilling for oil is important in Venezuela and Ecuador. There is much mining in Brazil, Bolivia, Peru, and Chile. Colombia is a world leader in platinum and the green gemstones known as emeralds. Venezuela holds diamonds and gold.

Life in the big cities of South America is much like life in the cities of North America. But many people outside of the cities live the way their ancestors lived, in tiny villages where there are dirt roads and no electricity. In the Amazon rain forest, many small groups of people still live by hunting and farming, as they have for thousands of years.

Over four hundred years ago, the empire of the Incas thrived in the Andes. Legend has it that the first Incas were created from the sun god on the Isle of the Sun in Lake Titicaca.

Weaving is an age-old art in the Andes, one passed down from generation to generation. People spin thick alpaca wool into yarn to make warm blankets, hats, and other clothing.

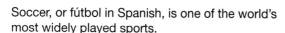

Soccer, or fútbol in Spanish, is one of the world's most widely played sports.

Oil Exported

Oil Fields

Coffee Bean Farming

Emerald Mining

Mining

Fishing

Shipping

Agricultural Area

The Amazon

Rubber

Mahogany Logging

Brazil Nuts Harvested

Cotton

Spanish-style Architecture

Indians of Peru

Agricultural Area

Machu Picchu (Inca Ruins)

Fishing in Lake Titicaca

Soccer

Mining

Anchovy Fishing

Brasilia

Mining

Light Industry

Rio de Janeiro

Mining

Trees Tapped for Tannin

Coffee Grown

Agricultural Area

Copper

Cattle Raising

Beef for Export

Fishing

Wheatlands

Bonito Fishing

Lumbering and Sawmills

Sheep Herding

South America

Countries and Cities

Ancestors of Native Americans crossed a narrow bridge of land between what is now Alaska and Siberia thousands of years ago. Over the centuries, these American Indians came to live all over North and South America. In the Andes, a Native American group called the Incas thrived and created a huge empire. Other American Indians created societies in other parts of South America.

South America was explored and conquered by Europeans after about

Suriname is an important producer of aluminum. Shown here is a factory that converts the ore into the metal.

Roads
Railroad

Barranquilla
Maracaibo
Caracas
Port of Spain
TRINIDAD AND TOBAGO
VENEZUELA
Georgetown
GUYANA
Paramaribo
SURINAME
Cayenne
FR. GUIANA
Santa Fe de Bogotá
COLOMBIA
Equator
ECUADOR
Quito
Guayaquil
Manaus
Belem
Fortaleza
PERU
BRAZIL
Rec.
Lima
Cuzco
La Paz
BOLIVIA
Brasilia
Salvador
Sucre
Belo Horizonte
Tropic of Capricorn
PARAGUAY
Antofagasta
Asuncion
Sao Paulo
Santos
Rio de Janeiro
Porto Alegre
CHILE
Cordoba
Mendoza
Rosario
URUGUAY
Valparaiso
Santiago
Buenos Aires
La Plata
Montevideo
Concepcion
ARGENTINA
Bahia Blanca
FALKLAND ISLANDS (U.K.)
Punta Arenas

58

1500. People from Spain, Portugal, and other European countries took over the land.

Today, South America's largest and most populated country is Brazil. More people live in Brazil than in all other South American countries combined. Argentina is the second-largest South American country.

Most South Americans speak the language of the European country that once ruled the area in which they live. For example, Brazil was once a colony of Portugal, and today most Brazilians speak Portuguese. Many other South American countries were once dominated by Spain, and Spanish is widely spoken on the continent. There are many American Indians in South America who speak the languages of their ancestors.

South America has many important cities. The biggest of them is São Paulo, Brazil, the third largest city in the world. Buenos Aires, Argentina, and Rio de Janeiro, Brazil, are also in the world's top ten in population.

Quito, Ecuador, is a very old city situated in the Andes. It is the capital and second largest city in Ecuador.

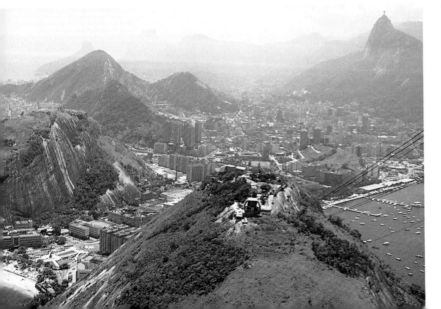

The second largest city in Brazil and one of the biggest in the world, Rio de Janeiro is popular with tourists.

Antarctica
The South Pole

Antarctica

Fifth largest continent
•
No permanent population
•
Highest mountain: Vinson Massif,
16,864 feet (5,140.14 meters)
•
Location of South Pole
•
Location of South Magnetic Pole
•
World's lowest recorded temperature:
Vostok, -129°F (-89°C)

SOUTH SHETLAND
ISLANDS

ATLANTIC OCEAN

LARSEN
ICE SHELF

Weddell Sea

ALEXANDER
ISLAND

ANTARCTIC
PENINSULA

*Bellingshausen
Sea*

RONNE
ICE SHELF

COATS LAND

QUEEN

ELLSWORTH
LAND

FILCHNER
ICE SHELF

Prime Meridian

MAUD

Vinson Massif

LAND

ELLSWORTH
MOUNTAINS

PENSACOLA
MOUNTAINS

MARIE
BYRD
LAND

WHITMORE
MOUNTAINS

ENDERBY
LAND

ROCKEFELLER
PLATEAU

QUEEN
MAUD
MOUNTAINS

+ South Pole

AMERY
ICE SHELF

ROSS
ICE
SHELF

Mt. Markham

AMERICAN
HIGHLAND

Ross Sea

McMurdo
Sound

VICTORIA LAND

WILKES LAND

Antarctic Circle

© 1979 Rand McNally & Co.

PACIFIC OCEAN

INDIAN OCEAN

+ South Magnetic Pole

Antarctica, the coldest continent on earth, rests right on the South Pole. It is so cold here that a person without the right kind of clothing would freeze to death in a matter of minutes.

Antarctica is without sunlight for part of the year. A visitor at the South Pole would enjoy six months of never-ending daylight during the summer, and six months of frigid, never-ending night during winter. Midsummer is in December here, and the dead of winter happens in July.

Even in the summer the sun gives the continent little heat. Most of Antarctica is covered with snow piled so thick it forms a mile-high heap at the South Pole. Bitter winds howl over the vast ice sheet.

Microscopic creatures teem in the waters around Antarctica, but large animals can be found there as well. Among these are seals, birds, and the blue whale. Antarctica is the home of many penguins. Though penguins are birds, they cannot fly. Their wings are used as paddles to help them move underwater. Today, no humans make a permanent home on this frozen continent, but hundreds of scientists study Antarctica's unique environment.

Penguins frolic in the cold waters off the coast of Antarctica. These are adélie penguins, one of only two species that breed in Antarctica.

World Facts and Comparisons

General Information

Mean distance from the earth to the sun, 93,020,000 miles.
Mean distance from the earth to the moon, 238,857 miles.
Equatorial diameter of the earth, 7,926.38 miles.
Polar diameter of the earth, 7,899.80 miles.
Mean diameter of the earth, 7,917.52 miles.
Equatorial circumference of the earth, 24,901.46 miles.
Polar circumference of the earth, 24,855.34 miles.

Total area of the earth, 197,000,000 square miles.
Total land area of the earth (incl. inland water and Antarctica), 57,900,000 square miles.
Highest elevation on the earth's surface, Mt. Everest, Asia, 29,028 feet.
Lowest elevation on the earth's land surface, shores of the Dead Sea, Asia, 1,312 feet below sea level.
Greatest known depth of the ocean, southwest of Guam, Pacific Ocean, 35,810 feet.
Area of Africa, 11,700,000 square miles.

Area of Antarctica, 5,400,000 square miles.
Area of Asia, 17,300,000 square miles.
Area of Europe, 3,800,000 square miles.
Area of North America, 9,500,000 square miles.
Area of Oceania (incl. Australia) 3,300,000 square miles.
Area of South America, 6,900,000 square miles.
Population of the earth (est.1/1/92), 5,491,000,000.

Principal Islands and Their Areas

Island	Area (Sq.Mi.)
Baffin I., Can.	195,928
Borneo (Kalimantan), Asia	287,300
Celebes (Sulawesi), Indon.	73,057
Corsica, France	3,352
Crete, Greece	3,189
Cuba, N.A.	42,800
Cyprus, Asia	3,572
Great Britain, U.K.	88,795
Greenland, N.A.	840,000
Hainan Dao, China	13,100
Hawaii, U.S.	4,034
Hispaniola, N.A.	29,300
Hokkaidō, Japan	32,245
Honshū, Japan	89,176
Iceland, Europe	39,800
Ireland, Europe	32,600
Jamaica, N.A.	4,200
Java (Jawa), Indon.	51,038
Luzon, Philippines	40,420
Madagascar, Africa	227,000
Mindanao, Philippines	36,537
Newfoundland, Can.	42,031
New Guinea, Oceania	309,000
Puerto Rico, N.A.	3,500
Sakhalin, Russia	29,500
Sardinia, Italy	9,301
Sicily, Italy	9,926
Southampton I., Can.	15,913
Spitsbergen, Norway	15,260
Sri Lanka, Asia	24,900
Taiwan, Asia	13,900
Tasmania, Austl.	26,200
Tierra del Fuego, S.A.	18,600
Vancouver I., Can.	12,079
Victoria I., Can.	83,897

Principal Lakes, Oceans, Seas, and Their Areas

Lake/Country	Area (Sq.Mi.)
Arabian Sea	1,492,000
Arctic Ocean	5,400,000
Atlantic Ocean	31,800,000
Baltic Sea, Eur.	163,000
Bering Sea, Asia–N.A.	876,000
Black Sea, Eur.-Asia	178,000
Caribbean Sea, N.A.–S.A.	1,063,000
Caspian Sea, Asia–Europe	143,240
Chad, L., Cameroon–Chad–Nig.	6,300
Erie, L., Can.–U.S.	9,910
Great Salt Lake, U.S.	1,680
Hudson Bay, Can.	475,000
Huron, L., Can.–U.S.	23,000
Indian Ocean	28,900,000
Mediterranean Sea, Eur.–Afr.–Asia	967,000
Mexico, Gulf of, N.A.	596,000
Michigan, L., U.S.	22,300
North Sea, Eur.	222,000
Ontario, L., Can.–U.S.	7,540
Pacific Ocean	63,800,000
Red Sea, Afr.–Asia	169,000
Superior, L., Can.–U.S.	31,700
Tanganyika, L., Afr.	12,350
Titicaca, Lago, Bol.–Peru	3,200
Victoria, L., Ken.–Tan.–Ug.	26,820
Yellow Sea, China–Korea	480,000

Principal Mountains and Their Heights

Mountain/Country	Elev. (Ft.)
Aconcagua, Cerro, Arg.	22,831
Annapurna, Nepal	26,504
Apo, Mt., Phil.	9,692
Ararat, Turkey	16,804
Blanc, Mont (Monte Bianco), France–Italy	15,771
Bolívar (La Columna), Ven.	16,411
Cameroon Mtn., Cam.	13,451
Chimborazo, Ecuador	20,561
Cook, Mt., New Zealand	12,349
Cristóbal Colón, Pico, Colombia	19,029
Dhaulāgiri, Nepal	26,810
Elbert, Mt., Co., U.S.	14,431
El'brus, Russia	18,510
Elgon, Mt., Kenya–Uganda	14,178
Etna, Mt., Italy	10,902
Everest, Mt., China–Nepal	29,028
Fairweather, Mt., Canada–U.S.	15,300
Fuji-san, Japan	12,388
Gannett Pk., Wy., U.S.	13,785
Gongga Shan, China	24,790
Grand Teton Mtn., Wy., U.S.	13,766
Grossglockner, Austria	12,461
Hood, Mt., Or., U.S.	11,239
Illimani, Nevado, Bol.	21,151
Iztaccíhuatl, Mex.	17,343
Jaya, Puncak, Indon.	16,503
Jungfrau, Switz.	13,642
K2 (Godwin Austen), China–Pak.	28,250
Kānchenjunga, India–Nepal	28,208
Kātrīnā, Jabal, Egypt	8,668
Kenya, Mt., Kenya	17,058
Kilimanjaro, Tanzania	19,340
Kommunizma, Pik, Tajikistan	24,590
Kosciusko, Mt., Austl.	7,316
Koussi, Emi, Chad	11,204
Lassen Pk., Ca., U.S.	10,457
Logan, Mt., Canada	19,524
Longs Pk., Co., U.S.	14,255
Margherita, Zaire–Uganda	16,763
Matterhorn, Italy–Switz.	14,692
Mauna Kea, Hi., U.S.	13,796
Mauna Loa, Hi., U.S.	13,680
McKinley, Mt., Ak., U.S.	20,320
Misti, Volcán, Peru	19,098
Mulhacén, Spain	11,424
Nānga Parbat, Pak.	26,650
Nevis, Ben, U.K.	4,406
Ólimbos, Greece	9,570
Orizaba, Pico de, Mex	18,406
Pikes Pk., Co., U.S.	14,110
Popocatépetl, Volcán, Mex.	17,887
Rainier, Mt., Wa., U.S.	14,410
Sajama, Nevado, Bol.	21,463
Shasta, Mt., Ca., U.S.	14,162
Toubkal, Jebel, Morocco	13,665
Triglav, Slovenia	9,393
Vesuvio (Vesuvius), Italy	4,190
Vinson Massif, Antarc.	16,864
Washington, Mt., N.H., U.S.	6,288
Whitney, Mt., Ca., U.S.	14,491
Wilhelm, Mt., Pap. N. Gui.	14,793

Principal Rivers and Their Lengths

River/Continent	Length (Mi.)
Amazonas–Ucayali, S.A.	4,000
Amu Darya, Asia	1,578
Amur, Asia	2,744
Arkansas, N.A.	1,459
Brahmaputra, Asia	1,770
Colorado, N.A. (U.S.–Mex.)	1,450
Columbia, N.A.	1,200
Congo (Zaïre) Africa	2,900
Danube, Europe	1,776
Euphrates, Asia	1,510
Ganges, Asia	1,560
Huang (Yellow), Asia	3,395
Indus, Asia	1,800
Irrawaddy, Asia	1,300
Lena, Asia	2,700
Limpopo, Africa	1,100
Loire, Europe	625
Mekong, Asia	2,600
Mississippi, N.A.	2,348
Missouri, N.A.	2,315
Murray, Australia	1,566
Negro, S.A.	1,300
Niger, Africa	2,600
Nile, Africa	4,145
Ohio, N.A.	981
Orange, Africa	1,300
Orinoco, S.A.	1,600
Paraguay, S.A.	1,610
Paraná, S.A.	2,800
Peace, N.A.	1,195
Pechora, Europe	1,124
Plata–Paraná, S.A.	3,030
Red, N.A.	1,270
Rhine, Europe	820
Rhône, Europe	500
Rio Grande, N.A.	1,885
Salween (Nu), Asia	1,750
São Francisco, S.A.	1,988
Saskatchewan–Bow, N.A.	1,205
Snake, N.A.	1,038
St. Lawrence, N.A.	800
Sungari (Songhua), Asia	1,140
Syr Dar'ya, Asia	1,370
Tarim, Asia	1,328
Tennessee, N.A.	652
Tigris, Asia	1,180
Tocantins, S.A.	1,640
Ucayali, S.A.	1,220
Ural, Asia	1,509
Uruguay, S.A.	1,025
Volga, Europe	2,194
Xingú, S.A.	1,230
Yangtze (Chang), Asia	3,900
Yellowstone, N.A.	671
Yenisey, Asia	2,543
Yukon, N.A.	1,770
Zambezi, Africa	1,700

Index